First steps to emotional literacy

The emotional literacy handbook
Promoting whole-school strategies
James Park, Alice Haddon and Harriet Goodman
1–84312–060–7

Nurturing emotional literacy
A practical guide for teachers, parents and those in the caring professions
Peter Sharp
1–85346–678–6

Intervening early
Promoting positive behaviour in the early years
Nicky Hutchinson and Hilary Smith
1–84312–135–2

Behaviour in the early years
Angela Glenn, Jacquie Cousins and Alicia Helps
1–84312–104–2

Promoting positive thinking
Building children's self-esteem, confidence and optimism
Glynis Hannell
1–84312–257–X

First steps to emotional literacy

A programme for children in the
Foundation Stage and Key Stage 1
and for older children who have
language and/or social
communication difficulties

Kate Ripley
Elspeth Simpson

Routledge
Taylor & Francis Group

LONDON AND NEW YORK

KH

First published 2007
By Routledge
2 Park Square, Milton Park, Abingdon, Oxon OX14 4RN

Simultaneously published in the USA and Canada
by Routledge
270 Madison Ave, New York, NY 10016

Routledge is an imprint of the Taylor & Francis Group, an informa business

Typeset in Bembo by Jayvee, Trivandrum, India
Printed and bound in Great Britain by Ben & Bain Ltd, Glasgow

British Library Cataloguing in Publication Data
A catalogue record for this book is available from the British Library

Library of Congress Cataloging in Publication Data
A catalog record has been requested for this book

ISBN10: 1–84312–415–7
ISBN13: 978–1–84312–415–3

7/29/08

To Peg and the girl who lost Pink Bun

For my father John W. Macleod: 'ach is e'n grádh as mó dhiubh so'
(1 Cor. 00:13).

Contents

Acknowledgements

With grateful thanks to the staff and pupils of Pinewood Infant School and Resourced Provision for Language Impairment. Particular thanks to Chris Creak, Pinewood Infant School and Paul le Feuvre, Amery Hill School for technical support and advice.

Artwork by Caroline Bletsis.

What's on the CD-ROM?

The CD-ROM included with this book provides a wealth of resources to help teachers, schools and LEAs become more familiar with the First Steps Programme. Download them, print them out, or use them on your interactive whiteboard – it's up to you!

1. Five assessment storybooks: Meet "Pink Bun"!

These fantastic assessment booklets have been specially designed for adults to read with young people. "Pink Bun" is hiding in the pictures and finding him helps to focus the children's attention and keep the assessment fun! At the end of the story, the adult asks five key questions and records the child's response. Their response will help assess how emotionally literate they are and what work still needs to be done with them to promote further emotional development.

2. A training video

This short video is great for training staff how to put the programme into practice and shows real-life intervention in action.

3. A PowerPoint training presentation

An excellent resource for LEAs and schools to ensure all staff are familiar with the First Steps Programme, what it can do and how to use it.

CHAPTER 1

An overview of the First Steps Programme

Target audience: who might find the programme useful?

- Teachers in Early Years and Foundation Stages;
- Area special educational-needs co-ordinators (SENCOs) and pre-school SENCOs for use in pre-school settings;
- Sure Start;
- Portage home visitors;
- Staff in nurseries and day-care provision;
- Teachers and other adults working with children who have language impairment, social communication difficulties and autistic spectrum disorder (ASD);
- Behaviour-support teams.

The structure of the First Steps Programme

The programme is divided into two sections. For Part I the focus is on intrapersonal skills: the ability to recognise, define, label and discuss our own feelings and emotions. Children learn to:

- recognise their own emotional states;
- use words to label a range of emotions;
- identify the triggers for their own emotional states;
- talk about past and future emotions;

As part of group discussion they:

- learn that other people experience similar emotional states;
- understand that the triggers for others may be the same as for themselves . . . or not.

The second part of the programme extends the range of emotions that children are able to recognise and discuss. It also turns the focus to the actions that might be triggered by strong states of arousal. Group discussion helps children to:

- recognise how they might choose to respond to different emotional states;
- review the range of responses that others might make in response to the same emotional trigger;

- consider the immediate consequences of different action choices in response to states of arousal both to themselves and to the other people who might be involved;
- consider the longer-term consequences of different choices of action.

Introduction to the First Steps to Emotional Literacy Programme

The importance of emotional literacy in the educational context

Learning to understand our own emotions and those of other people is a key part of becoming a socially competent person who is able to establish and sustain positive relationships with other people. The social, emotional and behavioural skills (SEBS) which are involved 'underlie almost every aspect of school, home and community life, including effective learning and getting on with other people' (DfES 2003). These skills have been variously described as emotional literacy, emotional intelligence and social and emotional competence. In the educational context, the terms 'emotional literacy' or 'social and emotional competencies' have been favoured rather than 'emotional intelligence', perhaps in an attempt to distance these ideas from that of intelligence as simply 'IQ'.

The Department for Education and Skills (DfES) guidance (2003) identifies a range of skills that children who have good social and emotional competences are able to bring to the learning experience.

- to be effective and successful learners;
- to make and sustain friendships;
- to deal with and resolve conflict effectively and fairly;
- to solve problems with others or by themselves;
- to manage strong feelings such as frustration, anger or anxiety;
- to recover from setbacks and to persist in the face of difficulty;
- to work and play cooperatively;
- to compete fairly and win or lose with dignity and respect for competitors.

These are already skills for life and so it is not surprising that the advantages of being emotionally literate extend beyond the educational context. Goleman (1996) reported that emotional literacy is a significant contributor to success in life as measured by a range of criteria, that it increases resilience to the stresses of targets and competition and plays a role in resistance to mental-health problems.

The development of children's SEBS is considered to be 'fundamental to school improvement' and the Every Child Matters agenda because it contributes to a range of relevant factors:

- greater educational and work success;
- improvements in behaviour;
- increased inclusion;
- improved learning;
- greater social cohesion.

The DfES guidance (2003) on the social and emotional aspects of learning (SEAL) offers a welcome whole-curriculum framework for all pupils in Foundation Stage. However, the first part of this curriculum, red level, assumes that children have already had early experiences at home that will enable them to discriminate and label basic emotional states. Not all children will have had or have been able to access these experiences and the First Steps Programme is designed to help such children. The programme has been structured to lead into the DfES curriculum and is, therefore, relevant to all children in Early Years and Foundation Stages. It is also relevant for older children who experience difficulties with language or who have an ASD.

The First Steps Programme was devised to support early social learning at a time when issues of behaviour, social inclusion and attendance are priority concerns within the education system.

Learning to understand emotions

Emotional literacy is defined as 'The ability to recognise, understand, handle and appropriately express (our) own emotions and to recognise, understand and respond appropriately to the expressed emotions of others' (Faupel 2003).

This definition makes it clear that children first learn about their own emotions and then progress to learning about the emotions of other people. This distinction between personal competences (intrapersonal skills) and social competencies (interpersonal skills) is recognised by the DfES in the Primary National Strategy: Developing Children's SEBS. Unfortunately, many social skills/emotional-literacy programmes assume that children have the necessary intrapersonal awareness and start the intervention with interpersonal skills. The First Steps Programme starts with the development of intrapersonal skills.

The first stages of learning to be emotionally literate start pre-school, in the home, when quality interactions take place between the child and his or her main carer. Small children may experience very strong emotions, but they have a limited ability to discriminate between them. 'A baby experiences global feelings of distress or contentment of discomfort or comfort' (Gerhardt 2004), but these feelings-states are not processed or labelled by the baby, who relies on adults to manage these states on his or her behalf. The baby or toddler can't make distinctions between feelings-states 'without help from those in the know' (Gerhardt 2004). The parent or carer helps the baby to become aware of his or her own feelings by using feelings-state talk.

With the support of feelings-state talk, children by the age of three are able to:

- use words to identify a range of emotions (Dunn and Brown 1991);
- talk about the triggers for emotions (Ridgeway and Waters 1985);
- talk about past and future emotions (Ridgeway and Waters 1985);
- talk about their actions that are triggered by emotional states (Ridgeway and Waters 1985);
- talk about the possible consequences of these actions (Ridgeway and Waters 1985).

The quality of feelings-state talk during the pre-school years can be related to the ability to understand the feelings of others at six years (Dunn and Brown 1991).

As many teachers in Foundation Stage are only too aware, a significant minority of children do not enter school with these skills in place. In addition, some children with specific conditions such as language impairment or ASD may not have been ready to learn the skills pre-school and may have particular difficulties acquiring these skills.

The First Steps Programme is appropriate for children in Early Years and for older children who may have had limited experience of feelings-state talk at home or who have specific conditions that have affected their ability to access feelings-state talk at an earlier stage in their development.

The aims of the First Steps Programme

- To replicate in a pre-school or school setting the early learning experiences of feelings-state talk that would usually take place in the home.

- To provide a programme that supports the DfES personal, social and health education (PSHE) curriculum framework for Foundation Stage by addressing issues of intrapersonal emotional learning (the p-levels to red level).

- To provide a programme that can be included in the reception year (YR) PHSE curriculum or as part of the literacy hour or in circle time.

- For the materials to be flexible for use with individuals or as part of small-group or whole-class interventions.

Learning emotional language helps children to understand emotions and talking about emotional states helps to manage and control emotions.

(Kopp 1989)

The programme

The First Steps Programme is designed to replicate in a school or pre-school setting the early learning experiences of feelings-state talk. Part I of the programme is in the form of a daily intervention and is intended to be limited to ten to twelve weeks.

Individual programme

The adults recruited to the programme observe a child who has been selected for the programme during the course of each day. The adults intervene with feelings-state talk when an incident occurs that prompts an emotional response from the child.

The programme includes a guide to using feelings-state talk and details about the features of feelings-state talk that research indicates makes it effective:

- frequency
- diversity
- context
- causal content
- consequences
- sample scripts of feelings-state talk as models for the process.

Group intervention

The group intervention is linked to the carpet time or circle time that is part of the routine for most settings at the end of a day. One or more children is invited to share their story about an emotion that they have experienced during the day. The feelings word that has been chosen is introduced to the whole group using the feelings-state picture for the word. When a child has told his or her story, structured questions are posed to the group about their experience of that emotion state and what happened to make them feel like that.

The programme includes ideas for class or group extension activities to support the generalisation of the ideas that have been expressed by the children. The programme also includes some original stories that describe only one emotion. These are supplied with the programme because most stories include mixed or changing emotional states that children at this stage of development find confusing. The resources section does provide a list of published story materials that the teachers working with the pilot programme found helpful, although it may be necessary to focus on one chapter or part of a story which expresses one core emotion.

The second part of the First Steps Programme is designed to extend the vocabulary of emotions and to develop the discussion about feelings to include possible courses of action in response to those feelings and the consequences of the choice of different actions to oneself and others. This part of the programme links in with other programmes designed to develop emotional literacy and social skills, including the red level of the Primary National Strategy. Unlike the first part of the programme, structured daily input is desirable but not essential.

In addition to details about the programme, the materials include:

- how to select children for the First Steps Programme using a behavioural checklist and the 'Pink Bun' story;
- guidance for the training of the staff team to deliver the programme;
- a supplementary programme for children who do have the emotional language but are reluctant to talk about their own emotions;
- an introduction to the programme which includes the theoretical and research background;
- lists of references, resources and ideas for extension activities.

Language is the road map we use to find our way through the uncharted territory of our emotions.

CHAPTER 2

The theoretical framework for the First Steps Programme

Emotional literacy

Learning to understand our own emotions and those of other people is a key aspect of becoming a socially competent person who is able to establish and sustain positive relationships with other people. The SEBS that are involved 'underlie almost every aspect of school, home and community life, including effective learning and getting on with other people' (DfES 2003). These same core skills have been variously described in terms such as 'emotional intelligence', 'emotional literacy' and 'social and emotional competence'.

The term 'emotional intelligence' originated with Gardner in 1983 (Gardner et al. 1995) who pioneered the concept of multiple intelligences. He widened the idea of intelligence beyond the conventional range of familiar abilities that are measured in tests of intelligence such as verbal and mathematical reasoning. He identified specialist intelligences such as musical or kinaesthetic intelligence and two types of personal intelligence: intrapersonal intelligence and interpersonal intelligence. These two abilities were described by Mayer and Salovey (1997) as emotional intelligence. They defined emotional intelligence as 'The ability to perceive accurately, appraise and express emotion; the ability to access or generate feelings which facilitate thought; the ability to understand emotion and emotional knowledge; the ability to regulate emotions to promote emotional and intellectual growth.'

The skills involved are well described by Mayer and Salovey in a way that is clearly relevant to an educational perspective. However, the distinction between intrapersonal intelligence and interpersonal intelligence is made less obvious in this definition. It is this distinction that is central to the First Steps Programme because intrapersonal understanding is the prerequisite for the development of interpersonal skills. Intrapersonal understanding represents the first stage in learning to become emotionally intelligent.

Intrapersonal intelligence involves having access to one's own feelings, being able to discriminate them, label them and then use the knowledge to inform behavioural choices. Interpersonal intelligence is the capacity to discern and respond appropriately to the emotions of other people. Most existing programmes that are designed to develop emotional intelligence focus upon the interpersonal aspects of this learning process.

The idea of emotional intelligence was brought into the popular domain in the UK by Goleman (1996). He argued that emotional intelligence could be more influential than conventional forms of intelligence for 'success' as defined in terms of career, educational achievement or personal fulfilment.

This gave an impetus to include aspects of social and emotional intelligence in an educational agenda and the interest in the creation of emotionally literate schools. The concept of emotional intelligence has been incorporated into the educational framework as schools have begun to address issues of challenging behaviour from a social learning perspective. However, in this process, the term 'emotional intelligence' has largely been usurped in the UK by the term 'emotional literacy', which is most often attributed to Steiner (1997). This term has, perhaps, been favoured by educationalists in the UK in an attempt to distance the ideas of personal intelligence from that of intelligence as measurable by an intelligence quotient (IQ).

Faupel (2003) has a useful definition of emotional literacy which preserves the distinction between intrapersonal and interpersonal skills: 'the ability to recognise, understand, handle and appropriately express their own emotions and to recognise, understand and respond appropriately to the expressed emotions of others.'

The use of the term 'emotional literacy' in this context carries an implication that the skills may be learned, although some children may need more support than their peers to develop the skills. It also promotes the idea that the competencies involved in becoming emotionally and socially skilled may be analysed and taught as part of a developmental programme.

The First Steps Programme focuses on the point in development when children first begin to discriminate between their emotions, to label them and to understand the triggers for them. The programme is about the intrapersonal phase of development and, as such, provides the missing link for those children who appear to benefit little from conventional social-skills programme that focus on interpersonal skills.

Emotional literacy in an educational context

The Healthy Schools Initiative (1998) acknowledged the link between social and emotional well-being and mental health. The evidence suggests that emotional literacy is one of the resilience factors that contributes to mental health (see Buchanan 2000). In 2003, the Primary National Strategy of the DfES included aspects of emotional literacy that were later dealt with in detail in the DfES *Advanced Guidance for Schools* (2003) about developing SEBS.

Emotional literacy is well represented in the outcomes for *Every Child Matters: Change for Children* (DfES 2004) and the legal framework for the associated reform is set out in the Children Act (2004).

Three of the five outcomes reflect the importance of emotional literacy in their aims:

1 To be healthy

- Be mentally and emotionally healthy.
- Have healthy lifestyles.

2 To enjoy and achieve

- Be ready for school.
- Attend and enjoy school.

- Achieve national educational standards at primary school.

- Achieve personal and social development and enjoy school.

3 To make a positive contribution

- Develop positive relationships and choose not to bully or discriminate.

- Develop self-confidence and successfully deal with significant life changes and challenges.

The DfES guidance (2003) identifies a range of skills that children who have good social and emotional competences are able to bring to the learning environment:

- Be effective and successful learners.

- Make and sustain friendships.

- Deal with and resolve conflict effectively and fairly.

- Solve problems with others or by yourself.

- Manage strong feelings such as frustration, anger or anxiety.

- Recover from setbacks and persist in the face of difficulty.

- Work and play cooperatively.

- Compete fairly and win or lose with dignity and respect for competitors.

In order to develop these skills effectively in their pupils, schools are envisaged as becoming emotionally literate environments that are supportive to the emotional health and well-being of both students and staff.

The development of children's SEBS is considered to be 'fundamental to school improvement' (DfES 2003) because it contributes to a range of relevant factors:

- greater educational and work success (Catalano et al. 2003);

- improvements in behaviour (Wells et al. 2003);

- increased inclusion (Epstein 1996);

- improved learning (Durlak 1995);

- greater social cohesion in school (Sharpe and Faupel 2002).

The evidence also suggests that the importance of being emotionally literate extends beyond the educational environment. Thus, for Goleman (1996) emotional literacy is a significant contributor to success in life (as measured by a range of criteria), increases resilience to the stresses of targets and competition and plays a role in resistance to mental-health problems.

The focus for SEBS training in schools has primarily focused on support for children who have already been identified as experiencing difficulties with the management of their emotions and their behaviour. There are many materials and programmes that have been published to meet the needs of this group. For example, *Anger Management* (Faupel et al. 1998) or *How to Deal with Feelings* (Rae 2003). Most of these programmes are targeted at older children in Key Stage 2 (for example, Bannerjee et al. 2004 or Faupel 2003).

The DfES guidance for the development of children's SEBS (DfES 2004b), SEAL, offers a welcome whole-curriculum framework for learning and teaching for all pupils, starting at Foundation Stage. However, the earliest stages of learning to be emotionally literate start in the home when quality interactions take place between a child and the main carer(s) that focus on discussions about emotional states. This sort of dialogue has been called feelings-state talk by Dunn and Brown (1991) and is a key feature of the First Steps Programme.

The first part of the Foundation Stage SEBS curriculum, red level, assumes that children have had these early experiences at home that will enable them to discriminate and label the basic emotional states. In fact, the first exercises go beyond recognising the basic emotional states such as happy, sad, angry and frightened and involve quite sophisticated concepts such as excited and surprised.

The First Steps Programme is designed to help children who have not fully experienced the early 'emotional-state talk' to access Foundation Stage PHSE curriculum, red level. The programme has been structured to lead into the DfES curriculum and is, therefore, relevant to all children in Early Years and Foundation Stage. It is also relevant to older children who experience particular difficulties with language or who have an ASD.

Background to the First Steps Programme

Learning to talk about feelings: self-awareness

For most children, the first stages of learning to be emotionally literate start at pre-school when quality interactions take place between the child and his or her main carer(s). Small children may experience very strong emotions, but they have a limited ability to discriminate between them. 'A baby experiences feelings of distress or contentment, of discomfort or comfort' (Gerhardt 2004), but these feelings-states are not processed or labelled by the baby, who, at this stage, also relies on adults to manage these states on his or her behalf. Babies also have a very limited repertoire of responses to their states of arousal, primarily laughing or crying, which are interpreted as showing intent by the adults around them who use context as their cues for guiding these interpretations. The baby or toddler cannot make distinctions between feelings-states 'without help from those in the know' (Gerhardt 2004). The parent or carer helps the baby to become aware of his or her own feelings by using feelings-state talk. The feelings are given verbal labels by the adult, who makes a judgement about the feeling that is being experienced, based on their understanding of feelings and their observations of the triggers for the baby/toddler's reaction.

There is evidence from neurological studies that the visceral experience of feelings is located in the amygala which is part of the limbic system. However, the ability to label and describe feelings is a language function, which is organised by the language centres in the neo-cortex. Clinically, we can observe the separation of these two functions by observing people who have a condition called alexthymia for whom these two aspects are not co-ordinated. They are able to experience feelings so, for example, they will cry in response to certain situations. However, they are confused and may be overwhelmed by a feeling because they are unable to define, label or explain it. Their response to the visceral experience is often to confuse the emotional pain with physical pain and to somaticise it so that they complain of physical symptoms.

Small children who have not yet learned to label their states of arousal may also be overwhelmed by strong feelings that they are unable to label, define or explain.

Children learn the language and feelings with the help of feelings-state talk that is experienced as part of the everyday interactions that take place between carers and children. Children who have difficulties with language, whether a specific language impairment, as part of global learning difficulties or as a component of an ASD, will find it more difficult to learn to label, define and explain their feelings of strong arousal and may continue to be overwhelmed by them beyond their early childhood.

Putting words to emotional experiences – matching the word to the visceral response – represents the first step towards emotional literacy. For most children, this learning will be part of their everyday, spontaneous interaction with a parent(s) or carer(s) before they start school. The importance of feelings-state talk in the development of a child's understanding of their own emotions and, subsequently, the emotions of other people was first highlighted by Dunn and Brown (1991). The significance of these 'conversations' in the development of shared meaning, theory of mind and interpersonal skills was further investigated by Denham et al. (1992).

Dunn and Brown (1991) found that from about twenty months children will use emotionally descriptive language in their interactions with family members. There is a rapid increase in children's vocabulary of emotions between twenty-four to thirty-six months and mothers and children also talk about the causes of emotions, particularly the toddler's own emotions (Dunn and Brown 1991). Ridgeway and Waters (1985) found that by thirty-six months children could talk about past and future emotions and could discuss the triggers for emotional states, their actions arising from these emotional states and the consequences of those actions.

This level of emotional understanding and awareness among the three-year-olds observed in these studies masked considerable individual differences, as professionals working with Early Years and Foundation Stage population would testify. Dunn and Brown (1991) found wide variations among the three-year-olds in the frequency with which feelings were talked about within the family. The variation affected all the key features of the dialogue, such as:

- diversity of themes;
- contexts in which the discussion took place;
- casual content;
- consequences of actions related to feelings.

The differences in discourse were systematically linked to differences in outcomes when the children were followed up at six years of age for their ability to make judgements about the feelings of others. Children who grew up in families where feelings-state talk was frequent were much better at making judgements about the emotions of unfamiliar peers in an affective perspective-taking task. In this sort of task, the children are asked questions about what people in standard situations might be feeling about what has happened. Most recent studies use picture stories or video material to explore affective perspective-taking, for example, Bannerjee et al. (2004).

It is interesting to note that children were more likely to be engaged in discussions about emotions and their causes when they were in dispute with others for some reason. We know not to attempt to engage older children in social discussions when emotions are running high, but the work of Dunn and Brown would suggest that for younger children social conflict has a role in the development of social understanding.

As many teachers in Foundation Stage are only too aware, a significant number of children do not enter school able to understand and manage their own emotions. These children will inevitably have difficulties understanding and managing their interactions with other children and research. Bannerjee et al. (2004) have indicated that these children are at risk of peer rejection, loneliness, low self-esteem and high levels of social anxiety. It is often this same group of children who engage in aggressive behaviour towards their peers and who later become the focus for anger-management groups in their schools. Some of these children will not have experienced quality feelings-state talk within their homes or day-care settings, while others may have specific conditions such as speech and language impairment or an ASD, which would affect their access to feelings-state talk during the pre-school years. The First Steps Programme aims to give teachers and adults in schools and pre-school settings a framework for delivering quality feelings-state talk in an educational environment. However, learning about our own emotions, how they make us feel inside, what triggers them, how to express them in socially acceptable ways and how to read and respond to the emotions of others is a life-long learning task.

From feelings-state talk to understanding feelings and behavioural control: self-regulation

Learning about the language of emotions is a powerful tool for understanding the emotions themselves (Kopp 1989). The concepts that we develop about our own internal states first help us to explain and manage our own behaviour and then to understand and predict the behaviour of others. Small children have simple concepts that relate to a limited range of emotions. Our concepts become more sophisticated over time and the development of metalinguistic skills helps us to understand the more abstract, subtle rules and mores that govern socially acceptable behaviour.

The research evidence shows that the use of the language of emotions in a dialogue with their parents or carers enables children:

- to state their own feelings (Hesse and Cicchetti 1982);
- to recognise the triggers for their own emotions (Bretherton et al. 1986);
- to understand feedback about feelings (Kopp 1989);
- to anticipate the consequences of how they express their feelings (Bretherton et al. 1986);
- to establish causal relationships between events and feelings (Hesse and Cicchetti 1982).

Once children have acquired these skills, they are able to begin to use the language of emotion to regulate their emotions (Bretherton et al. 1986). Self-talk about our own emotional states is an important component of managing our emotions and regulating our behaviour (Kopp 1989).

The quality of family discourse about feelings has been shown to be important in the development of social behaviour in children. Zahn-Waxler et al. (1979) showed that the way in which parents responded to their child when he or she caused hurt or distress to another child affects how the child will respond to other children when they are older and that the behaviour generalises across situations. It was the quality of the dialogue in terms of identifying how the other child felt and what might be done to make things better that affected the children's later responses to the distress or anger of others. The hypothesis is that family conversations about the emotional state of self and others helps to establish shared meanings about experiences. The identification of the triggers for our own feelings and sharing common triggers for emotions is a key component of the First Steps Programme that helps to develop this awareness of the feelings of others.

At an experiential level, it is natural to believe that the ability to understand the emotions of other people would lead to an empathy that would influence our behaviour towards them in a positive way. Most of the social-skills programmes that are carried out in primary schools are predicated on this assumption and provide external rewards for pro-social behaviour. However, on a cautionary note, some studies have found that having the skill to understand the feelings of others is no guarantee of friendly or pro-social behaviour towards them (Shantz 1983, Eisenberg 1986).

The rationale for the First Steps Programme

There are two key features of early social learning:

1 The ability to recognise and to label emotional states with the support of adults who are in tune with our needs. These adults would usually be key attachment figures and so insecure early attachments can affect the ability to access the first stages of emotional literacy.

2 The opportunity for facilitative dialogues with the main carer about our emotional states.

There are groups of children who may not easily access these relevant experiences pre-school for a range of reasons.

- In some families there is little of what Dunn and Brown (1991) would describe as feelings-state talk at home. Parents who have not experienced feelings-state talk for themselves may find it hard to interact in this way with their own children.

- Children who spend time in day nurseries where there is little individualised feelings-state talk may have limited compensatory opportunities for this to take place at home.

- Children who have social communication problems or an ASD who find it particularly hard to understand emotions may benefit from following the First Steps Programme for an extended period of time.

The First Steps Programme was devised to replicate the early pre-school learning experiences which are, for many children, a part of everyday family life, in a form that could be included in the PHSE curriculum or as part of the literacy hour. The programme has been designed to support children who have difficulty understanding their emotions and the emotions of others because they have missed some key learning opportunities before they started school.

Part I of the First Steps Programme

The programme follows the research evidence about how children develop the language of emotions and how they learn to use that knowledge to regulate their own behaviour and to understand the emotions of others.

The first stage, Part I, is to label the real emotions experienced by the children during their day and to talk about those emotions with the child at the time. Talking about 'real' emotions in the context in which they occur enhances the understanding of emotions (Denham 1992).

The real emotions that members of the group have experienced in the recent past are discussed. Ideally this would be done daily and would include the range of emotions experienced by the children during the day. Children as young as thirty-six months can talk about past emotions (Ridgeway and Waters 1985).

The discussion about these real situations helps to stimulate the use of emotional language. Questioning and repetition are important for stimulating the emotional language of children (Denham et al. 1992).

Learning emotional language is a powerful tool for learning to understand emotions and talking about emotional states helps us to manage/control these emotions (Kopp 1989).

The use of story material to generalise the discussions about emotional states is a key component as some children will find it easier to discuss emotions and to explore their consequences through a neutral character in a story. These experiences enable children to distance themselves from and to reflect upon emotional experiences (Bretherton et al. 1986). The results from the pilot study using the First Steps Programme indicated that there is a small group of children who have learned the language and the emotion but who find it hard to talk about their own emotions. A set of materials was subsequently developed to support children who find it hard to acknowledge their own emotions and who have difficulty dealing with their feelings.

Quality dialogues about emotions help children:

- to recognise the triggers for their emotions;
- to anticipate the consequences of how they express these emotions;
- to use emotional language to regulate their emotions (Bretherton et al. 1986).

This particularly applies to negative emotions (Dunn and Brown 1991). The feelings-state dialogues are structured as questions which are discussed during and after each story. The ability to understand and state their own feelings helps children:

- to understand feedback about the feelings of others;
- to establish causal relationships between events and feelings;
- to explain and predict the behaviour of others (Hesse and Cicchetti 1982).

Children need first to learn how to recognise, label, understand and express their own emotions (intrapersonal skills) before they are able to recognise, label understand and respond appropriately to the expressed emotions of others (interpersonal skills). The First Steps Programme starts with the intrapersonal skills which are the prerequisite for developing successful interpersonal skills.

The development of intrapersonal skills and discussions in a group setting about common triggers for emotions prepare the children for an understanding of the causal relationships between their actions and the feelings of others.

Part II of the First Steps Programme

In the second stage of the programme, Part II, children are encouraged to discuss the range of actions that might be triggered by different emotions. For each emotion experienced in a situational context the possible choices of action are identified. The situations may be based on the real-life experiences of the group or on carefully selected story material. Each possible action is discussed in turn with the key questions being focused on the consequences of the choice of that action.

- How will the actor feel?
- How will each of the other participants feel?
- What are the immediate outcomes of that action?
- What are the longer-term outcomes of that action?

The First Steps Programme is designed as an early intervention for children who might otherwise later experience difficult relationships with their peers. These children often find it hard to talk about their feelings, to take responsibilities for their actions and to predict the reactions of others to their behaviour. Because of these difficulties they may be included in social-skills training programmes such as anger-management courses which assume that they have a more sophisticated understanding of their own emotional states than is the case and as a consequence they may appear to gain little from such training.

CHAPTER 3

The selection of children for the First Steps Programme

Children will enter school in YR with very different pre-school experiences that may affect their ability to recognise, label and talk about their own feelings. How they attempt to manage their feelings will impact on their behaviour towards the adults and other children that they meet in school. The First Steps Programme is primarily intended as an individual intervention for children who have particular difficulties with the earliest stages of developing emotional literacy. The group activities are designed to reinforce the individual programme. The group and whole-class activities that are included in the programme underpin the red level of the Primary National Strategy: developing children's SEBS (DfES 2004).

Children are selected for the programme on the basis of:

- teacher observations;
- behavioural questionnaire;
- responses to questions using the 'Pink Bun' story format.

The information obtained from the assessments will establish the baseline data for each child and the assessment procedure should be repeated at the end of the time-limited intervention using the First Steps Programme. As with any other form of intervention, an evaluation is needed in order to demonstrate the effectiveness of the implementation of the programme.

Teacher observations

Teachers and classroom assistants are involved in ongoing observations of the children in their care. Some more structured observations are carried out and recorded in the entry profile when a child starts school (Foundation Style Profile, CCA 2003).

The entry profiles address social and emotional development as part of building a comprehensive picture of a child's strengths and they are regularly updated during the first year at school. The profiles, therefore, provide both information about a child when they enter school and a device for measuring progress in the six areas of development that are recorded on the profile. Strands within the first two areas of development are particularly relevant when considering children for a First Steps Programme:

1 Personal, social and emotional development (dispositions and attitudes, social development, emotional development);

2 Communication, language and literacy (linking sounds and letters, reading, writing);

3 mathematical development;

4 knowledge and understanding of the world;

5 physical development;

6 creative development.

A comparison with the assessments in the other areas of development can be useful when deciding whether a child has particular difficulties with the early stages of emotional literacy or is experiencing a more global delay in their development.

Teachers who are concerned about a child's social and emotional development may derive additional information by monitoring carefully their response to stories which have an emotional content. This type of story is scripted in the red level of the Primary National Strategy, where 'Ruby' experiences feelings of happy, sad, excited and scared at nursery. Responses to questions about the character's emotional state will help to identify those children who find it hard to recognise, label and talk about feelings. However, the story material presented in the First Steps Programme (to take the character in the 'Pink Bun' story as an example) presents only one emotion in each story because children in the early stages of the development of emotional literacy benefit from one, simple clear message and any ideas about changing and conflicting emotions are confusing for them at that stage of development.

The behaviour checklist

The behaviour checklist has been designed to supplement the information obtained from the entry profile and to be as quick as possible for teachers to complete. The questions have been selected to explore each of the five domains set out in the Primary National Strategy as indicated in Table 3.1.

Table 3.1

Personal competencies:	Social competencies:
Intrapersonal skills	Interpersonal skills
Self awareness	
	Empathy
Self regulation	
	Social skills
Motivation	

In the pilot study for the project, teachers were asked to complete the behaviour checklist for children whose social and emotional skills were developing well in order to provide a control group for the evaluations. Children in the control group presented a very different behavioural profile from the children who were struggling with the early stages of emotional literacy. The behaviour checklist is presented in Table 3.2.

Table 3.2

Behaviour checklist for teachers	YR	Date		
Name:	**True**	**Sometimes true**	**Not really true**	**Not true**
Tries to negotiate or try a different tactic when things go wrong.				
Will persist with a task even if it is hard.				
*Copes with defeat in a game or competition (no major sulks or tantrums).				
Will share toys and equipment.				
*Copes when can't get own way.				
Is sensitive to the feelings of others.				
Recognises the early signs of others being angry.				
Can label/name own feelings.				
Will accept consequences of own actions and does not blame others.				
Is liked by peers.				

*'Copes' = no sulks or tantrums

(Adapted from Faupel 2003)

It may be helpful for the behaviour checklist to be completed by all the adults who work with the child regularly as some children will show different behaviours with different adults and in different settings. Although the checklist is designed to record observations in a group setting, parents may like to comment about how their child responds at home as this will help to build up a more comprehensive understanding of how the child responds in different situations.

The behaviour checklist can be completed again by the same adults at the end of the time-limited first-steps intervention. It is important that people do not refer to their previous ratings before completing the checklist for the second time. Changes of ratings in a positive direction will indicate that the skills learned have begun to generalise into real-life settings.

Story-based assessments

A standard story format has been written to assess children's ability to recognise feelings, to use the language of feelings and to identify the triggers for those emotions. The 'Pink Bun' is hiding in the pictures and finding it helps to focus the children's attention and to keep the assessment fun. At the end of the story, the adult will then ask the five key questions and record the child's responses. The recording of the responses to the story is important in order to evaluate the child's progress when the 'Pink Bun' story is read again at the end of the intervention.

In the pilot study, the story assessment did identify a subset of children who were able to identify feelings, label them and identify the triggers but who were not able to talk about their own feelings. A modified version of the First Steps Programme was developed for this group of children and is presented as a separate section (see p. 49).

The story 'Pink Bun' and the five key questions are included in the programme pack.

Additional information

As discussed in the introduction to the programme, children may have had little access to feelings-state talk for a range of reasons. Parents will have valuable information about their child's early development and any family circumstances that might have affected the opportunities for conversations about feelings to take place at home. Some parents may want to know more about feelings-state talk and how they can help at home.

Children who have experienced early language difficulties may not have had the language skills to benefit from feelings-state talk during the pre-school years and support from their parents to implement and reinforce the programme would be particularly helpful. Some children may come to school with no obvious language problems and so it is always advisable to check the records for any involvement with the speech and language therapy services before they started school.

Children who have been identified as having an ASD are at high risk for difficulties in the area of recognising, labelling and identifying the triggers for their own feelings. These children will need more time than others to develop the intrapersonal skills before they are able to understand the interpersonal aspects of social interaction such as empathy. The First Steps Programme may still be appropriate for some children on the autistic spectrum in Key Stages 3 and 4.

Table 3.3

STORY ASSESSMENT

Name of child _____ **Date** _____

Assessed by _____

Read the assessment story 'Pink Bun'
Ask the following questions and record the child's response

Question	Child's response
What happened?	
How does Danny feel?	
What did Danny do?	
Have you felt sad like Danny?	
What made you feel sad?	

CHAPTER 4

Setting up a First Steps Programme

Once the senior management team of a school or pre-school setting has decided to use the first-steps programme it will be important to identify a programme co-ordinator. The programme co-ordinator may be a teacher who has children who might benefit from the programme, the SENCO, or a member of the school or setting management team. The programme co-ordinator will be responsible for:

- planning the implementation of the programme including the time limits for Part I of the programme;

- organising and delivering the awareness training;

- selecting the children for the intervention;

- training the adult team around the child;

- co-ordinating the implementation of the intervention including the monitoring and review meetings with the team around the child;

- evaluation of the intervention.

Sample time line

Term 1

At any time during Term 1:

- The senior management team takes the decision to use the First Steps Programme.

- A project co-ordinator is appointed.

- The project co-ordinator familiarises him/herself with the programme and prepares the materials for the awareness training.

- The project co-ordinator sets the date and time for the awareness training.

During the second half of Term 1:

- Awareness training takes place for the whole staff, parents and governors.

- Children who might benefit from the programme are identified by their staff team and discussed with the project co-ordinator.

- The project co-ordinator assesses the children who have been identified by their staff team using the behaviour checklist and the assessment story, 'Pink Bun'.

- The project co-ordinator, together with colleagues, decides which children to include in the programme.

- The project co-ordinator discusses the programme and its aims with the parents of the children who will take part in the programme.

- The project co-ordinator plans the training for the team around (each) child and sets the training date.

Term 2

- The project co-ordinator delivers the training to the team(s) around the child(ren).

- The adults agree a start date for Part I of the First Steps Programme.

- The programme is implemented for four/five weeks with the project co-ordinator available to support the adult teams.

- A review meeting of the members of the adult teams with the project co-ordinator is organised to discuss any issues and to monitor progress.

- At the end of the intervention, 8–10 weeks, the project co-ordinator carries out the re-assessments of the children.

- The project co-ordinator prepares a written evaluation of the project for the teams, the senior management, governors and parents.

- The adults involved in delivering the programme agree the next phase of the intervention.

Awareness training for the whole staff team

Schools and pre-school settings that are planning to introduce the First Steps Programme will need to inform all the staff and the parents of Early Years and Foundation Stage children about the aims of the programme. It is important to make clear that although only a small number of children will be selected for individual intervention, the whole-group, circle-time, activities will benefit all the children. Research indicates that all children in Foundation Stage will benefit from:

- talking about past and future emotions;

- learning that others experience similar emotional states;

- understanding that the triggers for others may be the same as for themselves ... or not.

These aspects of intrapersonal and interpersonal social skills are included in the aims of Part I of the programme.

Part II of the programme in which the range of emotions that are discussed are extended is clearly relevant for all children in Key Stage 1 as part of a process that continues into adult life. The emphasis on actions and their consequences is a component of a social learning agenda that links into social skills/PHSE programmes, such as the Primary National Strategy: Developing Children's SEBS (DfES 2004) and to a whole genre of social-skills programmes that aim to change behaviour which has been identified as aggressive or challenging.

The PowerPoint presentation, which can be found on the CD-ROM, has been used in various forms to introduce the programme to the school staff who were involved in the pilot project, to educational psychologists, to speech and language therapists and to academics at national and regional conferences. Chapter 2, which presents the theoretical framework for the programme, will provide the background information that a project co-ordinator might need in order to modify the slides to make the content relevant to his or her target audience. It may be appropriate to add slides that describe the setting and the reasons behind the decision to implement the First Steps Programme, as there are resource implications to this decision.

The discussion about the theoretical framework for the programme will also provide all the background information that a project co-ordinator will need in order to present the awareness-raising training.

Recruitment of the adult team

The project co-ordinator will have to identify the children who will be included in the programme before the staff team can be recruited. The staff team around each child will consist of the adults who interact with the child on a regular basis and who are in a position to observe the child's behaviour at first hand. If it is possible to include parents in the adult team, this will help to generalise the child's learning into different settings. Parents who have been recruited to the team will be able to use feelings-state talk at home and, thereby, extend the scope of key features of feelings-state talk such as the frequency, diversity and range of contexts in which the interactions take place.

In a school, the adult team might include the teacher, classroom assistants and midday supervisors together with the parents. These people will need to work together in order to implement the first part of the programme.

The programme co-ordinator is responsible for recruiting the team around the child and for explaining the programme to the child's parents if they are not actively involved.

Training the adult team

All the adults who have been recruited to the staff team will require training in order to implement the programme. The training would usually be planned and delivered by the programme co-ordinator.

Key components of the training

Background information

- An introduction to emotional literacy and its contribution to personal and social well-being.
- The intrapersonal skills that children would usually learn before they start school.
- How these key intrapersonal skills are learned using feelings-state talk.

The background information for this part of the training is presented in Chapter 2.

Learning to use feelings-state talk

The key feature of Part I of the First Steps Programme is the use of feelings-state talk in interactions with the children who are selected for the intervention. For most children, feelings-state talk is a component of the everyday interactions that take place at home between them and their carers without any specific training having taken place. It is a skill that is integral to 'good parenting' and would have been modelled in families over successive generations. Children who have, for a variety of reasons, experienced limited feelings-state talk before starting at school or nursery will be those who will benefit most from the First Steps Programme.

Training to use feelings-state talk in an educational setting will build on a natural skill that most parents use as a matter of course with their pre-school children. The training will help to make explicit a skill which the adults in the team may have used successfully in the past with their own children.

Feelings-state talk

The first step towards becoming emotionally literate is to be able to link our own subjective experiences of emotions to verbal labels that are shared by other people in our community. Once those labels have been attached to the feelings, it becomes possible to share our feelings with others and to understand that other people may share the same feelings. This process of learning the language of feelings would usually take place at home during the everyday spontaneous interactions that are shared by parents/carers and their children. These dialogues are known as feelings-state talk (Dunn and Brown 1991). Research shows that there is considerable variation between families in how often feelings are talked about. Children from families where feelings-state talk was frequent during the pre-school years were found to be much better at making judgements about the emotions of others (an interpersonal skill) at the age of six, (Dunn and Brown 1991).

The evidence suggests, therefore, that feelings-state talk is important in the early development of emotional literacy. The First Steps Programme was designed to replicate the pre-school learning experiences which are a part of everyday family life for most children, in a form that could be included in the PHSE curriculum for children in Foundation Stage.

Key principles for feelings-state talk

There are five key features of feelings-state talk that research indicates will contribute to its effectiveness.

1 Frequency

Feelings-state talk in the home might take place almost every time a child experiences and expresses an emotion. Even during a baby's nappy change adults may be verbalising sad/happy as a reflection on their child's implied emotional state. The frequency of the interactions is clearly related to the availability of the main carer(s). This may be physical availability, the amount of time spent in the child's company, but also emotional availability, giving full attention to the child – which might be compromised if the carer is stressed, very busy or depressed.

In a group setting, it will not be possible to observe and reflect on every emotion that a child might experience during a session. However, if a key worker is assigned to a child or a small number of children, it will be possible to offer individual feelings-state talk several times during a session.

2 Diversity

It is important to give feelings-state talk in response to a range of emotions and, particularly, to keep a balance between noticing comfortable and not-comfortable emotions. There is always the possibility that strongly expressed emotions such as fear may dominate feelings-state talk. It is important that adults using the programme are aware of this and make a conscious effort to balance between negative and positive emotions and address a range of emotions. For children who have had difficulties learning the language of emotions, it is important to start with the four basic emotions that are universally experienced and signalled non-verbally: sad/upset, happy, angry, scared/frightened. It is important that all people working with a child have agreed how each emotion will be verbally labelled – for example, 'upset' may be a more natural label than 'sad' for a small child who has fallen over.

3 Context

Quality home-based feelings-state talk will usually take place where the emotion was expressed and at the time when that emotion was experienced. The aim for adults using the First Steps Programme is to try to replicate this close alignment of 'where' and 'when', as the interaction will be more meaningful for the child and learning will be maximised.

4 Causal content

Identifying with the child what happened to trigger a particular emotional state is an important factor in helping children to understand their own emotions. Learning that certain triggers are linked to particular emotions is an early form of social learning and Hesse and Cicchetti (1982) suggest that children by three and a half are able to establish causal relationships between events and feelings. It is only when we can identify triggers for our own emotions (intrapersonal skill) that we can go on to recognise that other people share the same emotional responses to some situations as we do and develop empathy (interpersonal skill).

5 Consequences

Many children who have difficulties with the early stages of emotional literacy may not appear to understand the consequences of the actions which they take in response to their emotional states. The idea of cause and effect may not easily be established. The First Steps Programme includes activities to help children identify actions associated with different emotional states and share ideas about the possible consequences of the various action choices. Research (Bretherton et al. 1986) suggests that most children as young as three and a half are able to anticipate the consequences of how they express their feelings.

Children who have experienced quality feelings-state talk are able to use the language of emotion to regulate their emotions (Bretherton et al. 1986) and use self-talk to manage emotions and regulate their behaviour (Kopp 1989).

Using feelings-state talk in the First Steps Programme

Feelings-state talk would usually take place during spontaneous interactions between pre-school children and their parents or carers. The First Steps Programme offers a technique for replicating this early experience in an educational setting. All adults who have regular contact with the child are recruited to the programme and will have been trained to engage in feelings-state talk before the programme begins. The members of the adult team will observe the child(ren) during everyday activities in the classroom and at playtimes and lunchtimes. When an incident occurs that prompts an emotional response from the child, the adult follows a standard procedure:

- The adult observes an emotional response.
- The adult assesses the context of the response and watches the child's non-verbal and verbal communication around the event.
- The adult labels the feeling based on their assessment of the situation (to link the experience of that state of arousal with the feelings word).
- The adult talks about that feeling with the child and together they reflect on how the child's body is responding (to link the verbal label for that experience with the visceral response to that emotion).
- The adult talks with the child about what happened to make the child feel that emotion (to link the experience of the emotion to a particular event or trigger).

Together the adults in the team ensure that each child is engaged in feelings-state talk at least four times each day – the frequency principle. At the start of the programme it is possible that one emotional state may appear to dominate the child's experience. The team will try to observe and respond to a range of emotions for each child – the diversity principle. The adults will endeavour to respond spontaneously to the expressed emotional state of the child so that the dialogue starts immediately and where the incident happens – the context principle. The feelings-state talk will extend to focus on what happened to trigger the emotion – the causal context principle.

The first phase of the programme does not extend to a discussion of actions and their consequences. This extension is introduced when the adult team is satisfied that the child is able to label his or her feelings appropriately and to discuss the triggers for those feelings. In terms of the implementation schedule, this phase – the consequences principle – may be introduced after the first review period. However, the timing will depend on each individual.

Sample scripts for feelings-state talk

The members of the adult team will observe their target child(ren) during the course of each day and observe any events that precipitate an emotional reaction. When an emotional reaction is observed, the adult approaches the child and engages him or her in feelings-state talk.

It is important for people to have the opportunity to practise feelings-state talk as part of the training programme as well as watching scripts modelled on the CD-ROM. Research into the effectiveness of training in altering practice indicates the enduring relevance of the old (Chinese) proverb:

> I hear and I forget,
> I see and I remember,
> I do and I understand.

(i) Sample scripts

Four sample scripts of feelings-state talk are presented as models and can be used as practice scenarios (see Shanks 2003). The instructions for the activity might include:

- Work in groups of three and allocate three roles for the activity: the child, the adult and the observer.

- Select one of the scenarios, then the 'child' and 'adult' role play the script.

- The observer completes the checklist.

- The participants discuss the feedback from the observer.

- The participants swap roles until all three have had a turn as the child/adult/observer.

(ii) Writing a personal script

- Ask each person to complete the form (see Table 4.1) 'situations that precipitate emotional responses in your setting'.

- As a whole group, discuss the events and the emotions that are frequently triggered by those events.

- Ask each person to select one of their events and to write a short scenario based on their own experience and practice.

- Participants take turns to act the adult role for their own scenario, generating their own feelings-state talk script.

- The person in the observer role completes the checklist for each scenario and the three participants discuss the feedback for each scenario in turn.

Sample scripts for activity (i)

Example of script to discuss sadness and happiness

Adult: Who would like to share a time when they felt sad? Bethany would you like to say something about what happened to you last night?

Child: I lost my hamster, my brother left the cage open and he ran away.

Adult: Oh dear, how did you fell Bethany when you found out your hamster was lost?

Child: I cried and cried because I was really sad.

Adult: I'm sure you did. What did your body feel like when you were sad?

Child: It felt like someone was squeezing my heart until it hurt. It felt like I couldn't breathe properly.

Adult: Yes we do feel like that when we are upset; it feels like our chest is all tight. What else did your body feel like?

Child: I cried and that made my throat hurt too.

Adult: Poor you. Sometimes we have that funny feeling in our throat just before we cry don't we? Do you still feel sad?

Child: No, I feel happy now because I found my hamster. He was hiding in my shoe. When I put my shoes on this morning I found him. I felt really happy and I was jumping up and down and I couldn't stop smiling. I could feel my heart beating faster because I was so happy.

Adult: So, where is your hamster now Bethany?

Child: In his cage and mummy says my brother isn't allowed to open the cage again so we don't lose him again.

Plenary session to discuss a feeling

Adult: We've heard what happened to Bethany last night, has anyone else felt sad like that before and felt that their heart was being squeezed and that they couldn't breathe properly?

Adult: Jason would you like to share what happened to make you feel like that?

Child: I lost my mum when we were out shopping.

Adult: Oh dear that must have made you feel very sad.

Adult: What about you Jake?

Child: I cried when my brother broke my train set.

Adult: Has anyone got a story about when they felt happy like Bethany and felt like jumping up and down? Becky, what about you?

Child: I was really happy when my Nanna came out of hospital. Mummy said I had to sit quietly because Nanna was tired so I sat and gave her a cuddle and I felt all warm inside.

Modelling feelings-state talk

The CD-ROM, section two shows adults who were involved with the pilot study modelling interactions with children using feelings-state talk.

Table 4.1

Activity (ii)

Situations that precipitate emotional responses in your setting

Activity	Event	Emotion expressed
●		
●		
●		
●		
●		

Agreeing verbal labels for emotions

When they are using feelings-state talk, the adults will try to follow the lead of the child and interpret and label their expressed emotions based on the context cues that are available. However, it is important that the verbal labels that are to be used for at least the core emotions are agreed by all the adults who will be involved with a child. Alternative verbal labels will be confusing for a child who is learning to link his or her experience of an emotion with a verbal label.

The adult team might use the form (see Table 4.2) to identify the words that they commonly use to label the core emotions. The core emotions for the programme, the first to be learned and labelled are happy, sad, angry and frightened. The first-steps stories illustrate these core emotions. The alternative labels can be discussed and the team agree on the verbal label that will be used by them all.

Once the labelling of the core emotions has been well established, the team may wish to extend the programme to include other emotions that are frequently expressed in their setting. Those will need to be discussed in the same way so that all the adults are using the same verbal label for that emotion.

Table 4.2

Core emotions: form for discussion

Emotion	Alternative verbal labels	Label that will be used
Happy	• Is there a label that is used by the children that is current?	
Sad	e.g. unhappy	
Angry	e.g. cross	
Frightened	e.g. scared	

Extensions of the core emotions

• _____

• _____

• _____

• _____

• _____

Familiarisation with the First Steps Programme

Once the members of the adult team have practised feelings–state talk, the co-ordinator will review the aims of Part I of the programme and discuss the stages of the programme in detail. Part I of the programme is presented in Chapter 5.

At the end of the training, the co-ordinator will discuss the time scale for the implementation of the programme and the arrangements for review, monitoring and evaluation.

Questions that have been asked about using feelings-state talk

Some adults may be concerned that they have not labelled a child's emotional state 'correctly'. However, at this stage in the programme, the adults will only be using labels for the four basic emotions: happy, sad, angry, frightened, so there is less likelihood of misinterpretation than there would be when attempting to label more subtle nuances of emotion. The other important factor to bear in mind is that the adults in the team are only attempting to do what 'good' parents do, without necessarily having any meta-cognitive awareness that they are using feelings-state talk that will develop the emotional literacy of their child. Parents who use feelings-state talk as a regular feature of everyday interactions may make 'mistakes' in their interpretations from time to time, but this does not have any long-term consequences for the child.

Some of the children who have been selected for the programme may present as angry and, therefore, may be aggressive towards other children. It is hard for the members of the adult team around the child to ignore a child who might be upset in order to interact with the child who is on the programme. At such times, it will be important to remember that whatever the age and size of the child on the programme, they have been selected because their emotional development is delayed. They may, therefore, behave like a toddler when faced with social interactions and life events that other children are able to manage in a style more appropriate for their age. It is by the use of feelings-state talk that parents and carers develop the social and emotional skills of young children and it is by using feelings-state talk, appropriate to the level of their emotional development, that the adult team around the child can support the children selected for the programme. The adults in the team will need to adopt the style of a caring, warm, supportive parent towards a toddler when they engage in feelings-state talk with children who are on the programme and this may not always be easy if the child has been unkind to others in the group.

Any children who have been affected by an event that has prompted an emotional response from the child on the programme will need the support of an adult. This would be part of the normal routine for a school or pre-school setting. This support would not usually be given by the adult who was designated to use feelings-state talk with the child on the programme at that time because he or she will need input as promptly as possible (the context principle).

In practice, it has been found that adults are able to intervene at an earlier stage of any potentially difficult situation and thereby deflect crises. This is because of the role of the adult team as vigilant observers who are ready to respond promptly with feelings-state talk to the expressed emotions of children on the programme.

CHAPTER 5

The First Steps to Emotional Literacy Programme
Part I

Introduction

Part I

The first part of the programme is intended to be time limited, on average eight to ten weeks in duration. It consists of a daily routine which involves both an individual and a group-work component. The intervention focuses on the four core emotions that are experienced by all people in all cultural settings (see Figure 5.1).

HAPPY	SAD	ANGRY	FRIGHTENED

Figure 5.1

With the help of feelings-state talk, the children learn to identify their physical response to events and use feelings-state words to label that response. They also learn to link the feelings to the events that triggered them.

The project co-ordinator and the members of the adult team around the child will make the decision about when a child is ready to move from Part I to Part II of the programme. Some children may benefit from more than one cycle of intervention at Part I of the programme.

Part II

The second part of the programme consists of a group or whole-class intervention. The range of emotions that are discussed is extended so that the materials for the red level of SEAL will become a valuable resource at this stage. New feelings-state words are introduced in the same way as for the group component of Part I although some children may benefit from individual feelings-state talk to develop an understanding of their experiences of more subtle emotions.

This part of the programme helps children to discuss and evaluate the actions that they might take in response to their emotional reactions to events. The consequences that different courses of action might have for themselves and others are explored with the aim of helping them to become aware that they have choices about the actions they take. Children are encouraged to take courses of action that have a positive outcome for all the people involved – the win:win option.

The Daily Programme

The daily programme has two components:

1 An individual intervention using feelings-state talk

2 Group work involving a whole class or a group of children.

1 An individual intervention using feelings-state talk

The aims of the individual intervention are for children:

- to learn to recognise their own emotional states (how they feel inside);
- to use words to label the core emotions that they experience during the course of the day;
- to identify the triggers for the feelings that they have experienced during the day.

2 Group work involving a whole class or a group of children

The aims of the group work components are for children:

- to learn that others experience similar emotional states;
- to understand that the triggers for others may be the same as for themselves but they may also be different;
- to provide opportunities to talk about past and future emotions;
- to develop the ability to discuss feelings with adults and other children.

Work with individuals

The project co-ordinator will discuss each child who has been selected for the intervention with the team around that child. The adults will all have received training in how to use feelings-state talk before the intervention begins. It is helpful for the members of the staff team to have some key information about each child they will be working with. The child vignette might include:

- names of family members, other significant adults, pets, friends;
- strengths and what the child enjoys doing at home and school;
- the areas of difficulty indicated in the behavioural checklist;
- the aims of the intervention for the child.

The adult team will all begin the intervention on an agreed date. Throughout each day, the members of the adult team will observe the child as he or she engages in a range of activities in the classroom, on the playground, at lunchtime and breakfast club, at the after-school club, if these are also part of the child's daily experience.

When an incident occurs that prompts an emotional response from the child, the adult who makes the observation will take the opportunity to interact using feelings-state talk.

i. The adult will go to the child as soon as possible, so that the feelings-state interaction starts as close in time and in the same physical area in which the event took place. This is the context principle.

ii. The adult analyses the context of the response and the non-verbal and verbal communication of the child. The adult labels the feeling that the child is experiencing based on their assessment of the total situation linking the experience of that state of arousal with the feelings-word

iii. The adult talks to the child about how they are feeling in terms of how their body is responding linking the visceral response to the verbal label for the experience

iv. The adult talks to the child about what happened to make them feel that way linking the experience of the emotion to a particular event or trigger. This is the causal principle.

v. The adult does what is necessary to ensure that the child is calm and comfortable if a negative emotion has been triggered. Only when the child is restored to a comfortable state, withdraw.

It is important for the adults in the team to try to respond to a range of emotional states that each child experiences during the day. If a child is often angry and, therefore, aggressive towards the other children, it is important to balance feelings-state talk about anger with interactions around the other emotions, even if it means the observer being even more vigilant to seize the appropriate moment. This is the diversity principle.

During this part of the programme, it is important that the adults in the team around the child ensure that each child experiences feelings-state talk at least four times each day. This is the frequency principle.

In order for each child to have a consistent experience of feelings-state talk from a number of different adults, it is important for all the adults to follow the basic five steps. The adult style during the interaction should be the calm, warm and supportive approach of a caring parent to a younger child (toddler age) because this is the emotional development age of the children who will have been selected for the project. This may not always be easy if the child has hurt or upset another child who needs comforting – but by another adult.

Work with the class or a small group

During the course of the day, members of the adult team will record their interventions using feelings-state talk. A sample form is presented in Table 5.1 and may be photocopied.

Table 5.1

Name:		Date:
Child (initials)	**Feeling**	**Context for the feeling**

At a convenient time during the afternoon, members of the staff team share the interventions that they have carried out. The team co-ordinator then selects one emotion to be the focus for the end-of-day discussion for the whole group. The co-ordinator may choose an emotion that has been expressed by more than one child, an emotion that has not been the focus of discussion before or a particularly powerful emotion that has been expressed that day.

The first few weeks of the programme will concentrate on the four basic emotions that are experienced by children across the world and in all societies: happy, sad, angry, frightened. A wider range of more subtle emotions are introduced into the end-of-day plenary at a later stage. There will be children in the whole class group who have benefited from feelings-state talk at home and these children would be starting to discriminate the feelings expressed in the words used in the red level of the Primary National Strategy such as 'welcome', 'worried', 'belonging' and would not, therefore, have been selected for inclusion in the First Steps Programme. Although the ability of this group of children to discuss a range of feelings is more sophisticated than that of the target group, they too will benefit from whole-group discussion about feelings and:

- will develop the ability to discuss past and future emotions with adults and other children;
- will learn that other people experience similar emotional states;
- will understand that the triggers for others may or may not be the same as for themselves.

Most teachers will draw all the children together on the carpet before they go home and the feelings-state discussions can easily be incorporated into this daily routine. The group discussion follows a standard procedure each day:

- The team co-ordinator selects one of the emotions that has been experienced by a child on the programme during that day.
- The feeling word that has been chosen is introduced to the group using the feelings-state picture for that word. The pictures are included with the programme and may be copied.
- One of the children who has experienced that emotion is asked if they would like to share their story.

The adult will help the child to tell their story giving as much support as they need. Some children may not feel confident at first about telling their story and the adult may need to take the major part, pausing for confirmation from the child at key moments in the story. Group discussion will help all the children to:

1 develop the ability to discuss feelings with adults, other children. (If more than one child has experienced the same emotion, the team co-ordinator may decide to invite more than one child to tell their story.)

2 learn that others experience similar emotional states. (Ask other children in the group if they have ever felt like the child who has just told the story. Elicit ideas about how their bodies felt at the time.)

3 firmly link the body's (visceral) response to the label for that emotion. (For each individual 'story' ask the child what happened to make them feel like that.)

4 Understand that other people may share common triggers for the same emotional state, but also that their triggers may be different.

It is important for children to have the opportunity to discuss their own experiences, but sometimes reading a story about the emotion that has been chosen may be a useful supplementary activity. In most books there are a succession of emotions that are experienced by the characters in the same story or chapter. This is also true for the 'Ruby' story in the red level of the Primary National Strategy as she experiences the emotions of happy, excited, scared and sad within the space of a few lines. At the very early stages of learning about emotions, it is important that the messages are kept simple and clear. The stories which form part of this programme take each of the four basic emotions as a theme for a separate story. The stories are on the CD-ROM and may be copied and enlarged into a 'Big Book' format for class work.

When discussing the personal stories that children have contributed or when discussing story books with an emotional content, it is important to cover five key questions as part of the discussion:

1 What happened to trigger the emotion?

2 How did _____ feel inside?

3 What did _____ do? (Try to elicit an emotional response here, rather than an action.)

4 Who has felt like _____?

5 What made you feel like that?

The questions may be found at the end of each of the first-steps story books.

Figure 5.2

The pictures reproduced here are on the CD-ROM and may be photocopied and enlarged. They are intended to be used to introduce the feelings-state word of the day at the start of the whole class or in small group discussions.

Extension activities for the whole class or group

Sharing stories

1 Collect from the library a selection of stories that describe the four basic emotional states.

| HAPPY | SAD | ANGRY | FRIGHTENED |

2 Select parts of each story that illustrate only one of these emotions to use with the children when one or more of them has experienced that emotion during the day. (Note: try to avoid introducing more than one emotion or mixed emotions at this stage of the programme.)

3 Read the relevant story and ask the following questions.

- What happened?
- How did _____ feel?
- What did _____ do? (Elicit an emotional response not an action here – for example, 'cried'.)
- Who has felt _____ like _____ ?
- What made you feel _____ ?

Some books that are particularly helpful are listed in the Appendix.

Sharing triggers for emotions (i)

1 Read a feelings–state story to the children and ask the following questions:

- What happened?

- How did _____ feel?

- What did _____ do? (Elicit an emotional response not an action here – for example, 'cried'.)

- Who has felt _____ like _____ ?

- What made you feel _____ ?

2 Record on a chart the triggers for the feelings that the children identify

- What made you feel _____ ?

3 Make an illustrated feelings chart of things that make us feel ———.

| Angry | Sad | Happy | Frightened |

Figure 5.3

Sharing triggers for emotions (ii)

1 Read a feelings-state story to the children and ask the questions:

- What happened?
- How did _____ feel?
- What did _____ do? (Elicit an emotional response not an action here, for example, 'cried'.)
- Who has felt _____ like _____ ?
- What made you feel _____ ?

2 Discuss with the group or class.

- What made you feel _____ ?

3 The children draw their experiences. Some children may want to add text or captions to their drawings.

4 Put the drawings in a file that children can look at when they feel _____.

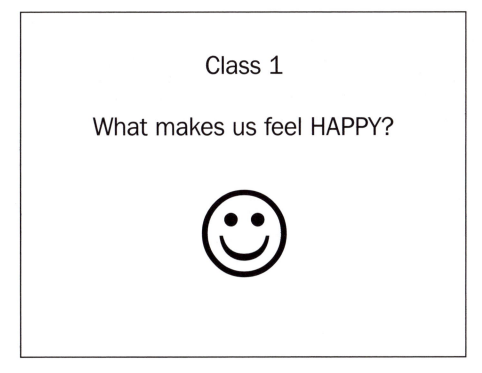

Figure 5.4

Activities for developing emotional awareness

Role play

1 Choose a story to illustrate a feeling that the children have discussed during the week.

2 Read the story and ask the following questions about the story:

● What happened?

● How does _____ feel?

● What did _____ do?

3 Role play the story, using the classroom dressing-up box. Ask each character in the story:

● What happened?

● How do you feel?

'Walk the Walk' role play

For children who have particular problems with empathy, try 'Walk the walk' role play. Each child has a turn to play each character in the story. This is particularly powerful if the stories are 'scripts' based on real-life events that the target child has experienced. They act the part from the perspective of themselves and any other children and/or adults who have been involved in the incident. The standard key questions are answered from the point of view of each person in the drama.

Puppets

1 Choose a story to illustrate a feeling that the children have discussed during the week.

2 Read the story and ask the following questions about the story:

● What happened?

● How does _____ feel?

● What did _____ do?

3 The children make stick puppets or finger puppets for each character in the story. Alternatively, use the puppets that you have in school and dress them up to be the characters in the story.

4 Set up a puppet theatre and act the story.

5 Talk about each character in the story:

● What happened?

● What did _____ feel?

● What did _____ do?

Figure 5.5

Personal stories

1 The children talk about what has happened to them. Either they tell their story or the adult tells their story or helps them to tell their story.

- What happened?
- How did you feel?
- What did you do?

2 The adult facilitates shared storytelling about that feeling using the structure of the narrative approach:

- Who (the characters)?
- Where (the setting for the story)?
- What happened (the sequence of events for the story)?
- How does _____ feel?

3 Collect the facilitated stories about each of the four core feelings (happy, sad, angry, frightened) in a separate story book.

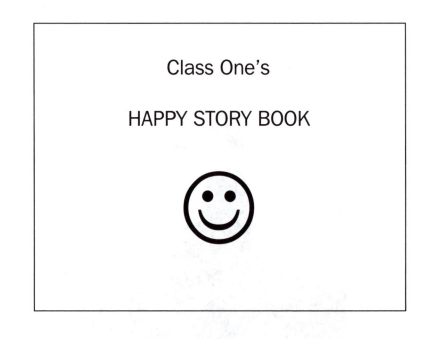

Class One's

HAPPY STORY BOOK

Figure 5.6

CHAPTER 6

The First Steps to Emotional Literacy Programme
Part II

Introduction

The second part of the programme builds on the first part by using the same learning process whilst extending the range of emotions that the children learn to label and discuss. This stage of the programme also turns the focus towards the actions that are made in response to the emotions that are experienced. The group and whole class discussions explore the consequences of different courses of action and encourage children to make socially appropriate choices. The aims may be summarised in terms of the continuation of the aims of Part I of the programme:

- to extend the range of emotional states that children are able to recognise and label, using feelings-state talk when appropriate;

- to identify the triggers for this range of emotions in themselves and others;

- to recognise that triggers for these emotions may be the same for themselves as for others;

- to further develop the ability to discuss feelings with adults and other children.

Part II of the programme focuses group discussions on:

- the actions that are triggered by emotional states;

- an exploration of the consequences of different courses of action for themselves and other people who are involved in a situation;

- an evaluation of the possible choices in terms of the best outcome for all concerned – a win: win option whenever possible.

Extending the vocabulary of emotions

Part I of the programme focused on the four basic emotions that may have an innate basis: happy, sad, angry or frightened. As children develop their emotional awareness they will learn that feelings vary in intensity and that there are words to express subtle differences in meaning. Table 6.1 is derived from the work of Bannerjee et al. (2004) and presents some of the nuances of emotions.

Table 6.1

Basic emotion	Extensions	Notes
Happy ☺	Glad Joyful Excited Ecstatic Pleased	
Sad ☹	Despair Grief Wretched Disappointed Miserable Upset	
Anger	Annoyed Irritated Cross Mad Furious	
Fear	Frightened Worried Nervous Anxious Scared	

Two other universal emotions may be included in the programme at this stage.

Surprise	Amazed Interested Fascinated Stunned	
Disgust	Horrible Yucky Gross	

Other emotions that children may experience and need to label in order to discuss them do not fit neatly into the extensions of these basic emotions. For example, anticipation may be linked to happy, sad, angry or frightened, according to the circumstances that surround the emotional experience. Jealousy may involve elements of sad as well as angry. Excitement may be tinged with a fear of the unknown.

In order for children to identify the emotions and to establish a shared meaning for the verbal labels that are used in their culture group, it is important to relate the feelings words to their own direct experiences of that emotional state. This means that when new feelings-state words are introduced, some children may need to experience individual feelings-state talk in response to events in their own lives.

The introduction of new emotional language may, therefore, follow the same process as Part I:

- individual feelings-state talk based on individual emotional experiences;
- group discussion to explore the visceral responses and situational triggers for the new emotional label that has been selected.

The choice may be based on the experience of individuals who agree to tell their 'story' or the group response to a joint experience such as the excitement generated by a visiting theatre group.

Introducing a wider range of vocabulary for feelings

1 Choose an emotion selected from the real-life experience of the children, which has been discussed in the group. Select a story that illustrates the feeling that the children have discussed. Try to introduce only one feelings state and no mixed feelings when you first introduce a new label.

2 Read the story and ask the questions about the story as for Part I:

- What happened?
- How does _____ feel?
- What did _____ do?
- Who has felt like _____ ?
- What made you feel _____ ?

3 Identify the common triggers for the new feelings-state as for the core emotions in Part I.

Feeling-word webs

1 Take each of the core emotions in turn using real-life or story-book material to introduce the feeling that is chosen.

2 For each emotion, ask the children if they can think of other words that people use when they feel happy, sad, angry or frightened.

3 Draw a feelings chart for the class as a group exercise. It can later be made into a display chart, if appropriate.

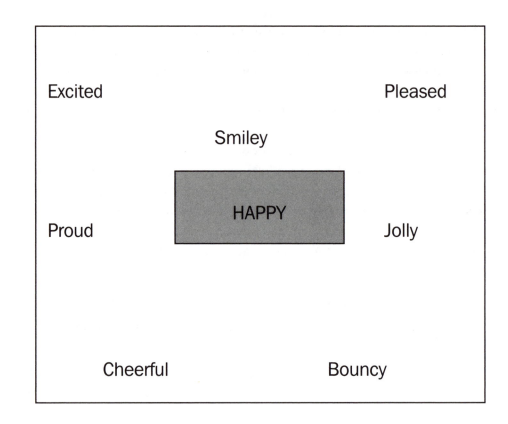

Figure 6.1

Introducing mixed emotions

1 The new words around each of the core emotions are put on cards and mixed up.

2 Children select which feelings chart to put them with.

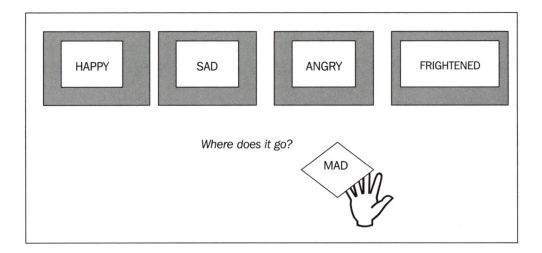

Figure 6.2

3 Some choices, such as 'mad' may be simple. Other choices may not be so obvious and the decision may depend on having more situational or context cues. The adult facilitator will describe one or two scenarios which would help to guide different choices.

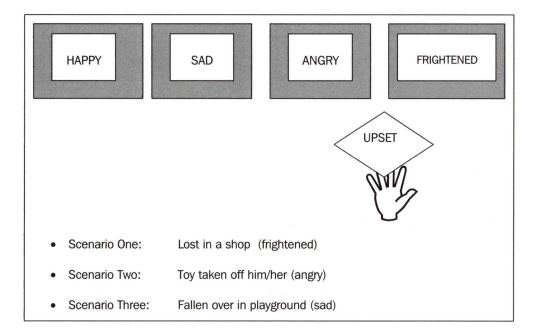

Figure 6.3

Class charts and books to illustrate new feeling words

1 Use the words that have been generated from the feelings-state charts. Take each of the new feelings-state words in turn, for example 'excited'.

2 Children discuss the triggers for feeling excited.

3 Children draw/write about what makes them feel excited. They can make picture books and story books about what makes the members of the class feel excited.

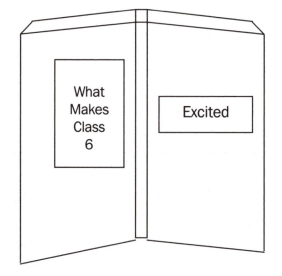

Figure 6.4

Actions and consequences

For this part of the programme, it is helpful to start with the first four universal emotions which will, by this stage, be very familiar to all the children. The process may be carried out in an individual, small group or class setting and be based on real-life or story-book material.

1 Take each feeling in turn and for each feeling ask, 'What did J do?'

2 Link the feeling to the action: 'J hit C because he was angry'.

3 Identify the trigger for the action: 'Why was J angry? C had taken his car away'.

4 Construct a choice board (see Figure 6.6).

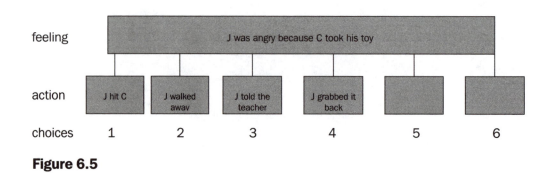

Figure 6.5

5 Discuss the action choices for J (these are generated by the children).

6 For each choice of action that has been suggested by the children, discuss the outcomes for J. What does J want to achieve – his car back or some other outcome?

7 For each action decide:

- Does J get his needs met?

- How does J feel?

- What are the consequences of that action for J?

- Will he get into trouble?

- How will he feel then?

- Are there longer-term consequences of the action?

- What are the outcomes for the other characters in the story?

8 For each character discuss the following key questions:

- Do they get their needs met?

- How do they feel?

9 Using the choice board, decide on the most effective action in terms of making people feel good and getting their needs met.

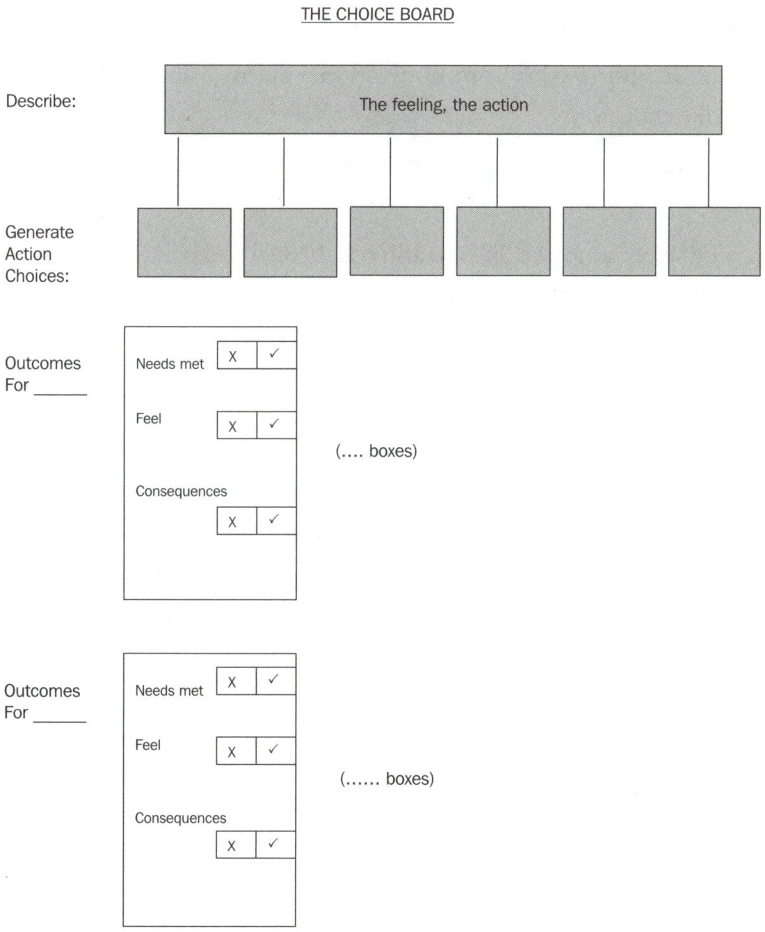

THE CHOICE BOARD

Figure 6.6

Activity 1 Mood pictures

1 Take pictures of the adults in the school that the child knows well.

2 Ask the adults to make the facial expressions for the basic emotion states.

3 The children sort the pictures to make sets according to:

- the person, regardless of the emotion depicted – for example, Mrs X looking angry/sad/happy/frightened, etc. – to show that we all express a range of emotions;

- the emotion that they are portraying – do we all look the same when we are happy/sad/angry/frightened?

4 The children talk about the possible triggers for the emotions depicted by the adults. Are the triggers the same for adults and children?

Activity 2 Reading expressions and body language

1 Children select a feelings-state card. An adult helps them to make the facial expression of that feelings-state. The use of modelling, when the adult makes an expression for the child to copy and using a mirror to give visual feedback to the child are often a great help with this.

2 Once the children can signal the emotions, they select a card, make the expression and the other children try to guess the emotion on the card.

3 To enhance the non-verbal communication, repeat, using body language cues as well as facial expression.

4 The adult models the appropriate body language and children practise with the help of a mirror.

5 The children select an emotion card and use the facial expression and body language for the others to guess what is on their card.

Activity 3 Role play of emotions

1 Use role plays of scripts that the children have written with the teacher of familiar stories and scenarios based on real-life situations that illustrate characters experiencing different emotions. The role plays can take the form of mimes of familiar stories.

2 The other children guess which story is being acted out. There may be pictures of the stories or story titles available to help the children guess.

3 Start with two possible choices and then extend the range.

There are several commercially produced series of pictures of emotions which are listed in the list of useful resources.

CHAPTER 7

Supplementary programme for Part I

Part I of the First Steps Programme is designed as a eight- to ten-week intervention in school to replicate the feelings-state talk that many parents do during the pre-school years as a natural part of their parenting style. This level of intervention is a positive experience for all children and even the most emotionally literate members of the group will benefit from the group discussions.

Children with special needs, particularly in the areas of speech and language impairment, social communication or those with an ASD may benefit from a slower pace of delivery of Part I of the programme. The language that is used in discussions and feelings-state talk will need to be modified to match the level of their language comprehension. The standard programme is, therefore, designed to benefit a wide range of children during Early Years.

The supplementary programme was devised to meet the needs of children who are able to recognise emotional states but who have difficulty discussing their own feelings. During the course of the pilot study it became evident that there was a small group of children who were able to identify and label emotions and to respond to the first three questions of the 'Pink Bun' assessment story, 'What happened?', 'How does Danny feel?' and 'What did Danny do?'

However, they were reluctant to relate the feelings to themselves and their own experiences: 'Have you ever felt sad like Danny?', 'What made you feel sad?'

Some of these children may have emotional difficulties that merit further investigation by professionals in the support services, such as educational psychology or the Child and Adolescent Mental Health Team.

The Supplementary Programme is not designed as a therapeutic tool but as an extension of the programme. A series of stories was written to support children who appeared unable to acknowledge or to discuss their own emotional responses. The stories were based on the same principles as *Social Stories* (Gray and Leigh-White 2002) but have a focus on the identification of an emotional state, rather than on supporting situations that the child finds difficult to manage.

The teacher and the staff team work very closely with the parents. It is particularly important for this group of children that the parents are as fully involved with the programme as possible.

The stories were presented in A4 size and the digital camera was used to take pictures of the child and his or her classmates to illustrate each part of the story. Each element of the story was presented on a separate page. The stories did include what the child could choose to do in response to the emotional state and so incorporated elements of both Part I and Part II of the First Steps Programme.

When Jim was cross

One afternoon at Oakwood School it was time for play.

'I want you to put your coats on', said Mrs Jones.

The children went to fetch their coats.

'It's very cold today children, you must do your coats up before you go outside', said Mrs Jones.

Jim put his coat on but he couldn't do it up.

Jim saw that all the children had done up their coats and gone out to play.
He couldn't go out because he hadn't done his coat up.

Jim was cross because he couldn't do his coat up.
He was so cross he forgot that he could ask for help.

He pulled a cross face and folded his arms.
He felt very cross.

'Come on Jim', said Mrs Smith, 'don't be cross'.
'I can't do my coat up', said Jim, 'It's a stupid coat'.
Mrs Smith asked Jim if he would like some help.
Jim remembered he could ask for help.
'Yes please', said Jim.

Mrs Smith helped Jim to do up his coat and Jim was able to go out to play.
He didn't feel cross anymore because he had remembered to ask for help.

Jim went out to play. He played on the bikes.

The feelings-state story approach was also used to help children who had difficulty managing their strong emotions beyond the range of the four basic emotions. They were effective in helping children to label a wider range of subtle feelings. The story for 'excited' is included as a model for this approach (see 'When Jim was Excited').

Stories were also used to encourage positive behaviour such as being kind and to illustrate how children can affect the emotions of others by their behaviour. Modelling the targeted behaviour for the pictures after the real event helped to reinforce the positive actions of one boy helping another with his painting apron and putting up his hand to answer a question.

The opportunity to read and reread examples of positive behaviour did help children like Jim to see themselves in a positive way and contributed to the raising of their self-esteem. Two stories are presented as examples of how behaviour can be modelled and reinforced: 'When Jim was Kind' and 'When Mrs Simpson was Pleased'. Names can be substituted and digital photos can be inserted to tailor the stories to individual settings.

When Jim was excited

Once upon a time there was a little boy named Jim.

Supplementary programme for Part I

> Insert a picture of 'Jim' and his Mummy and Daddy

He lives in Oakwood with his Mummy and Daddy.

He went to Oakwood Infant School.

> Insert a picture of Mrs Jones and Jim in class

Jim was in Mrs Jones's class.

One day when Jim came to school he was feeling very excited.

Insert a picture of Jim running around

He bounced about the classroom and was very noisy.

'Why are you so excited?' asked Mrs Jones.

Insert a picture of Jim with Mrs Jones

'Wait and see', said Jim.

Mrs Smith asked Jim to sit in the quiet room with the other children. Jim bounced into the quiet room and was very noisy.
'Why are you so excited?' asked Mrs Smith.

Insert a picture of children sitting quietly – not Jim. Mrs Smith with Jim

'Wait and see', said Jim.

Mrs Simpson came to the class to teach some signing. Jim bounced about the room and was very noisy.
'Why are you so excited?', asked Mrs Simpson.

Insert a picture of Jim with Mrs Simpson in the class

'Wait and see', said Jim.

Soon it was dinner time.

Insert a picture of children lining up ready to go for lunch

When the children got to the hall, Jim was very excited.
He bounced into the hall and ... gave his mum a big hug.
Jim's mum was the new school cook.

Insert a picture of Jim hugging his mum

'So that's why you were so excited', said Mrs Jones and Mrs Smith and Mrs Simpson.

When Jim was kind

One day Jim was at Oakwood school.
The children were sitting in the quiet room with
Mrs Jones.
'Today we are doing to do some painting',
said Mrs Jones.

Insert a picture of Mrs Jones showing the class a painting

'I am going to choose some children to go with
Mrs Smith to paint a picture'.
Mrs Jones chose Martin and Jim to paint first.
The boys went to the cloakroom to put their aprons
on.

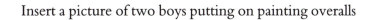

Insert a picture of two boys putting on painting overalls

'I can't do my apron up', said Martin.

Quick as a flash Jim said, 'I'll help you Martin'.
And he helped Martin to do up his apron.

Insert a picture of Jim helping Martin with his apron

'Thank you Jim', said Martin.
'Thank you for helping Martin', said Mrs Smith, 'That was very kind of you'.

When Mrs Simpson was pleased

One day Mrs Simpson came to Jim's class to teach some signing.

Insert a picture of children entering the quiet room and sitting down

All the children went into the quiet room and sat down in a circle.
Mrs Simpson had some symbols.
She showed the children some symbols.
'Who knows what this symbol says?'
asked Mrs Simpson.
Jim put up his hand and waited quietly to be chosen.
'Yes Jim', said Mrs Simpson.
'I think it means "where" ', said Jim.
Then Jim showed Mrs Simpson the sign for 'where'.
'Well done Jim', said Mrs Simpson, 'You remembered to put up your hand and not call out. That makes me really pleased'.

Insert a picture of Mrs Simpson looking pleased

CHAPTER 8

Ideas for more activities

Book Bank

General titles

Many traditional tales deal with a range of emotions

Hissey, J., Old Bear series. London: Red Fox

Various titles including:

(1991) *Old Bear and his Friends*

(1998) *Old Bear*

(2002) *Old Bear's All-Together painting*

Hughes, S., (2004) Alfie series. London: Red Fox

Various titles including:

Alfie and the Birthday Surprise

Alfie Gets in First

Alfie Gives a Hand

Alfie's Feet

An Evening at Alfie's

Hughes, S., (1993) *Dogger*. London: Red Fox

Jeram, A., (2003) *Contrary Mary*. London: Walker Books

Happiness

Ahlberg, A., (1990) *Happy Worm*. London: Walker Books

Blake, Q., (2005) *Angel Pavement*. London: Red Fox

Castle, C., (2003) *Happy!* London: Red Fox

Clark, G., (2002) *Max and the Rainbow hat*. London: Anderson Press Ltd

Graham, Bob., (2005) *Oscar's Half birthday*. London: Walker Books

Jarrett, C., (2004) *The Best Picnic ever*. London: Walker Books

Wadell, M., (2005) *You and Me Little Bear*. London: Walker Books

Waddell, M., (2005) *Let's go home Little Bear*. London: Walker Books

Worry

Wadell, M., (2002) *Tom Rabbit*. London: Walker Books

Ironside, V., (1998) *The Huge Bag of Worries*. London: Hodder & Stoughton

Wells, R., (2004) *Felix and the Worrier*. London: Walker Books

Excitement

Birchall, M., (2003) *What kind of monster?* London: Anderson Press Ltd

Dodds, S., (2002) *Is That You, Father Christmas?* London: Walker Books

Jealousy

Clark, G., (2002) *Nervous Norris: The Tale of a Dog - And a Cat* London: Anderson Press Ltd

Dunbar, J.,(2004) *The Secret friend.* London: Walker Books

Holabird, K., (2001) *Angelina on stage.* London: Puffin

Steptoe, J., (1997) *Mufaro's Beautiful daughters.* London: Puffin

Sadness

Chichester-Clark, E., (2004) *Up in Heaven.* London: Anderson Press Ltd

Chichester-Clark, E.,(2005) *I love you Blue Kangaroo.* London: Anderson Press Ltd

Clark, G., (2004) *Eddie and Teddy.* London: Anderson Press Ltd

Hayes, S., (2004) *Mary Mary.* London: Walker Books

Macdonald, A., (1993) *Little Beaver and the Echo.* London: Walker Books

Nimmo, J., (2004) *The Night of the Unicorn.* London: Walker Books

Rosen, M., (2004) *Michael Rosen's Sad book.* London: Walker Books

Varley, S., (1984) *Badger's parting gifts.* London: Andersen Press Ltd

Fear

Alborough, J., (2004) *It's the bear!* London: Walker Books

Alborough, J., (2005) *Watch out! Big bro's coming!* London: Walker Books

Birchall, M., (2005) *Rabbit's party surprise.* London: Anderson Press Ltd

Brown, R., (1981) *A Dark, Dark Tale.* London: Anderson Press Ltd

Browne, A., (2005) *Into the Forest.* London: Walker Books

Castle, C., (2003) *Happy!* London: Red Fox

Foreman, M., (2004) *Surprise, Surprise.* London: Anderson Press Ltd

Glicksman, C., (2005) *Big Black Dog.* London: Walker Books

Hicks, B.J., (2004) *Jitterbug Jam.* London: Hutchinson Children's Books

Ray, Jane., (1999) *Hansel and Gretel.* London: Walker Books

Waddell, M., (1992) *Owl Babies.* London: Walker Books

Waddell, M., (2005) *Can't you sleep Little Bear?* London: Walker Books

Anger

Carle, E., (1982) *The Bad Tempered Ladybird.* London: Puffin

Nimmo, J., (2004) *The Stone Mouse.* London: Walker Books

Oram, H., (2004) *Angry Arthur.* London: Red Fox

Love

Chichester-Clark, E.,(2005) *I love you Blue Kangaroo.* London: Anderson Press Ltd

Hill, E., (2005) *Spot loves his Dad.* London: Frederick Warne

McBratney, S., (2000) *Guess how much I love you.* London: Walker Books

Resources

Amos, J., Viewpoints series Cherrytree Books

Various titles including:
(1996) Honest
(2000) Kind: Two stories seen from Two Points of View
(2002) Fair
(2002) Reliable

Amos, J., Good and bad series. Cherrytree Books

Various titles including:
(2000) Hello
(2001) Cheat
(2001) Liar
(2001) Moody
(2001) Selfish

Amos, J., (2003) Problem solvers series. Cherrytree Books

Various titles including:
Why fight?
Why lose your temper?
Why be bossy?
Why tease?

Amos, J., (2003) Good Friends series. Cherrytree Books

Various titles including:
(2003) Don't say that!
(2003) It's mine!
(2003) Go away!
(2003) Move over!
(2003) It won't work!

Amos, J., Growing Up series. Cherrytree Books

Various titles including:
(2000) Being Helpful
(2000) Making friends
(2000) Being Kind
(2000) Sharing
(2000) Taking turns

Resources

Color Cards, *Emotions*. Bicester: Speechmark Publishing Ltd

Moseley, J., Materials to support circle time. *www.qualitycircletime.co.uk*

Pragmatics/Semantics; 1 Emotions/Facial Expressions (card set) Keighley: Black Sheep Press

DfES (2005) *Social and Emotional Aspects of Learning (SEAL)*. London: Department for Education and Skills

LCP., *PSHE & Citizenship Resource File*. Leamington Spa: LCP

References

Bannerjee, R., Daines, R., Watling, D. (2004) *Children's Social Behaviour Project Emotional Literacy Curriculum for Key Stage 2*. Brighton and Hove: Children and Families Directorate.

Bretherton, I., Fritz, J., Zahn-Waxler, C., and Ridgeway, D. (1986) 'Learning to Talk about Emotions: A Functionalist Perspective', *Child Development*, 57: 529–48.

Buchanan A. (2000) 'Present Issues and Concerns', in A. Buchanan and B. Hudson (eds) *Promoting Children's Emotional Well-Being*. Oxford: Oxford University Press, pp. 15–46.

Catalano, R. F., Berglund, L., Ryan, A. M., Lonczak, H. S. and Hawkins, J. (2002) 'Positive Youth Development in the United States: Research Findings on Evaluation of Positive Youth Development Programmes', *Prevention and Treatment*, 5.

Denham, S. A., Cook, M., Zoller, D. (1992) ' "Baby Looks Very Sad": Implications of Conversations about Feelings between Mother and Pre-Schooler', *British Journal of Developmental Psychology* 10: 301–15.

Department for Education and Skills (1998) *Healthy Schools: National Health Schools Standard Guide*. Nottingham: DfES Publications.

Department for Education and Skills (2003) *Advanced Guidance for Schools*. Nottingham: DfES Publications.

Department for Education and Skills (2004a) *Every Child Matters: Change for Children*. Nottingham: DfES Publications.

Department for Education and Skills (2004b) *Developing Children's Social Emotional and Behavioural Skills: A Whole Curriculum Approach, Primary National Strategy*. Nottingham: DfES Publications.

Dunn, J., and Brown, J. (1991) 'Family Talk about Feelings States and Children's Later Understanding of Others' Emotions', *Developmental Psychology*, 27: 448–53.

Durlak, J. (1995) *School Based Prevention Programmes for Children and Adolescents*. London: Sage.

Eisenberg, N. (1986) *Altruistic Emotion, Cognition and Behaviour*. Hillsdale, NJ: Lawrence Erlbaum Associates.

Epstein, T. and Elias, M. (1996) 'To Reach for the Stars. How Social/Affective Education Fosters Truly Inclusive Environments', *PH1 Delta Kappan* 78 (2): 157–62.

Faupel, A. (ed.) (2003) *Emotional Literacy: Assessment and Intervention Ages 7–11*. London: nferNelson.

Faupel, A., Herick, E., and Sharp, P. (1998) *Anger Management: A Practical Guide*. London: David Fulton.

Gardner, H., Kornhaber, M., Wake, W. (1995) *Intelligence: Multiple Perspectives*. London: Harcourt Brace.

Gerhardt, S. (2004) *Why Love Matters: How Affection Shapes a Baby's Brain*. London: Brunner-Routledge.

Goleman, D. (1996) *Emotional Intelligence: Why It Can Matter More than IQ*. London: Bloomsbury.

Gray, C. and Leigh-White, A. (2002) *My Social Stories Book*. London: Jessica Kingsley.

Hesse, P., and Cicchetti, D. (1982) 'Perspectives on an Integrated Theory for Emotional Development', in D. Cicchetti and P. Hesse (eds) *Emotional Development*. San Francisco, Calif.: Jossey-Bass, pp. 33–48.

Kopp, C. B. (1989) 'Regulation of Distress and Negative Emotions: A Developmental View', *Developmental Psychology* 25: 343–54.

Kuczaj, S. A. (1985) 'The Acquisition of Emotion Descriptive Language', *Developmental Psychology* 21: 901–8.

Mayer, J., and Salovey, P (1997) 'What is Emotional Intelligence?', in P. Salovey and S. Shulter (eds) *Emotional Intelligence and Emotional Development*. New York: Basic Books, pp. 24–38

Rae, T. (2003) *Dealing with Some More Feelings: An Emotional Literacy Curriculum*. Bristol: Lucky Duck Publishing.

Ridgeway, D. and Waters, E. (1985) *Emotional Literacy Group*. Southampton: Southampton City Council LEA.

Shanks, B. (2003) 'Only a Story?' *Speech and Language Therapy in Practice*, 233 (spring): 10–23.

Shantz, C. U. (1983) 'Social Cognition', in J. H. Flavell and E. M. Markman (eds) *Handbook of Child Psychology*. Vol. III. *Cognitive Development*. New York: Wiley, pp. 495–555.

Sharp, P., Faupel, A. (eds) (2002) *Promoting Emotional Literacy: Guidelines for Schools, Local Authorities and Heath Services*. Southampton: Southampton City Council.

Steiner, C. and Perry P. (1997) *Achieving Emotional Literacy*. London: Bloomsbury.

Weare, K. (2004) *Developing the Emotionally Literate School*. London: Paul Chapman.

Wells, J., Barlow, J., and Stewart-Brown, S. (2003) 'A Systematic Review of Universal Approaches to Mental Health Promotion in Schools', *Health Education* 4.

Zahn-Waxler, C., Radke-Yarrow, M., and Kind, R. A. (1979) 'Child-Rearing and Children's Prosocial Initiations towards Victims of Distress', *Child Development*, 48: 319–38.

Index